TUPPENNY STUNG

BY THE SAME AUTHOR

POETRY
No Continuing City
An Exploded View
Man Lying on a Wall
The Echo Gate
Selected Poems
Poems 1963-1983
Gorse Fires

AS EDITOR
Causeway: The Arts in Ulster
Under the Moon, Over the Stars: Children's Poetry
Further Reminiscences: Paul Henry
Selected Poems: Louis MacNeice
Poems: W.R. Rodgers

TUPPENNY STUNG
Autobiographical Chapters

MICHAEL LONGLEY

1994
Lagan Press
Belfast

Published by
Lagan Press
PO Box 110, Belfast BT12 4AB

The publishers wish to acknowledge the financial assistance of
the Arts Council of Northern Ireland in the production of this book.

© Michael Longley, 1994

ISBN No: 1234567890
Author: Michael Longley
Title: Tuppenny Stung: Autobiographical Chapters
Format: Paperback (126 x 196 mm)
1994

for Douglas Carson

Acknowledgements

'Tuppenny Stung' first appeared in the *Poetry Review*, vol.74, no.4, January 1985, edited by Mick Imlah;

Part I of 'The Empty Holes of Spring' was written for the Derek Mahon Special Issue of the *Irish Universities Review*, Spring 1994, edited by Brian Donnelly; Part II was one of several contributions to 'The Belfast Group: A Symposium', the *Honest Ulsterman*, No. 53, November/December 1976, edited by Frank Ormsby;

'Blackthorn & Bonsai' was delivered as a lecture in Trinity College, Dublin, on 16 July 1992, at the closing plenary session of the annual conference of the International Association for the Study of Anglo-Irish Literature;

'River & Fountain' was commissioned by Trinity College, Dublin, as part of the Quatercentenary commemorations and read aloud in the Public Theatre at the ceremony to mark the College's Charter Day on Friday, 13 March 1992.

My heart rouses
  thinking to bring you news
    of something

that concerns you
  and concerns many men. Look at
    what passes for the new.

You will not find it there but in
  despised poems.
    It is difficult

to get the news from poems
  yet men die miserably every day
    for lack

of what is found there.
  Hear me out
    for I too am concerned

and every man
  who wants to die at peace in his bed
    besides.

—William Carlos Williams

Contents

Foreword	11
Tuppenny Stung	13
The Empty Holes of Spring	31
Blackthorn & Bonsai	43
River & Fountain	77

Foreword

Each of these chapters was written in response to a commission. Editors and conference organisers suggested topic and theme. Even this compilation is the brain-child of Patrick Ramsey who runs the Lagan Press and Damian Smyth of *Fortnight*. It's not that I'm modest or nervous about attracting attention. No. I believe that "autobiography is at once the discovery, creation and imitation of the self"; that even the most self-centred narrative will include other people; that everyone's life-story helps to diminish in a small way the fear and ignorance that lead to fratricide in disputed territory such as ours.

When he was editor of the *Poetry Review*, Mick Imlah invited me to write about my childhood in south Belfast. 'Tuppenny Stung' released emotions that had gone underground. 'The Empty Holes of Spring' combines some reminiscences of Trinity days and my friend Derek Mahon, with a rather tetchy account of Philip Hobsbaum's Group, the former my most recent piece and the latter an echo from 1976: my contribution to a symposium in the *Honest Ulsterman*, it tried to correct some misconceptions about The Group, but undervalued the benificence of Hobsbaum who was instrumental in getting Macmillan to publish my first collection. The longest chapter, 'Blackthorn & Bonsai', could have been longer still, but it began life as a lecture to an international audience, and I guessed that a retired bureaucrat's Northern Irish version of *Barchester Towers* was unlikely to hold their attention for more than fifty minutes. I was honoured by an invitation from Trinity College, Dublin, to compose a poem in commemoration of the Quatercenenary. Autobiographical in every detail, 'River & Fountain' made me try new things in verse and thereby extend myself.

Thanks to this particular enterprise I now wonder if there will be more chapters, other stories, further discoveries and extensions. There's a lovely passage in George Moore's masterpiece *Hail and Farewell* which suggests why he went on and on: "The present is no more than a little arid sand dribbling through the neck of an hour-glass; but the past may be compared to a shrine in the coign of some sea-cliff, whither the white birds of recollections come to roost and rest a while, and fly away again into the darkness. But the shrine is never deserted. Far away up from the horizon's line other white birds come, wheeling and circling, to take the place of those that have left and are leaving."

TUPPENNY STUNG
Growing up in Belfast

I

I began by loving the wrong woman.

In 1936, when she was seventeen, Lena came from County Fermanagh to work for my parents as a maid. At approximately 4 pm on July 27 1939 I was born, followed half an hour later by my twin, Peter. My sister Wendy was nine when we arrived. According to her we were cranky babies, victims of the now discredited Truby King method of feeding by strict regime rather than demand. We did not get enough milk and because we yelled day and night were kept in separate rooms and prams—one at the back of the house, the other in the porch at the front. My mother concentrated on Peter, the slightly more difficult child. Lena looked after me and turned into my mother. She exchanged the uniform of a maid for that of a nurse, but this was for her much more than a promotion. She was a natural and devoted surrogate mother: the two of us became inseparable.

The Second World War began in September. My father who had survived the trenches enlisted again and was posted to England where he remained for two years. My mother, Lena and a succession of wayward maids looked after Wendy and 'the Twins' (as we were called until puberty, when we changed to 'the Boys'). The crying stopped as soon as we graduated to solids; and some photographs show us peacefully sharing a large black pram. Because those years are mostly beyond my recall, I have to borrow Wendy's memories of the air-raids on Belfast, the search-lights, the hand-bells and whistles, the gas-mask into which Peter and I were inserted, the perspex visors through which we peered and tried to make sense of the huddle under the stairs. There survive in my mind the rough feel of khaki as I climbed over a soldier's knee, the coolness of the brass buttons, the kitchen light reflected in the polished toecap of an army boot. Had the maid been bringing her soldier boyfriend home?

Just down the road from our house the King's Hall, a huge Art Deco concrete and glass barn, was converted into a barracks for the troops. One of them, Bill Hardy, married Lena, and they left Belfast for Nottingham in 1941. I was inconsolable and for weeks afterwards toddled to the front door when the bell rang, expecting Lena to be there. The marriage was not a success. With her daughter Paddy, Lena returned in 1945 to live with us for a few more years. The three of us accepted Paddy as a sister and I liked it when she called *our* father Daddy. As my love for Lena deepened, my relationship with my mother grew more tense and complicated.

I last met Lena in 1967 when, on her way to visit relations in Fermanagh, she called briefly to meet my wife and our first child. My arms melted around her in acceptance and surrender. She was (and, so far as I know, still is) working as a priest's housekeeper in New York. A few years ago Paul Muldoon and I gave a reading there in the Public Theatre. I had thought of contacting Lena, but was anxious that no audience would turn up and that she would be upset and embarrassed on my behalf. The evening turned out to be a considerable success. Lena should have been sitting in the middle of the front row.

II

My parents came from Clapham Common to live in Belfast in 1927. My father was a commercial traveller for an English firm of furniture manufacturers, Harris Lebus. Before the war his territory was the whole of Ireland, and the family album is full of his photographs—Antrim, Donegal, Kerry: he seems quickly to have fallen in love with the island. Business did not resume until well into the fifties; so on leaving the army my father for several years scraped a living as a professional fundraiser—for the Ulster Hospital for Women and Children and, when the introduction of the National Health Scheme rendered him redundant, for the War Memorial Rebuilding Fund. The inventiveness and panache of his schemes were a minor talking-point in the community. Photographs of him receiving cheques and smiling at Ulster's grandees appeared regularly in the local press. He was always referred to as Major R.C. Longley, M.C., a billing he disliked. The war was over, he used to insist. But Ulstermen adore military titles and my father's, with its aura of courage as well as authority, endured stubbornly. To this day when certain people hear my surname, which is unusual in Northern Ireland, they ask "Any relation to the Major?"

As a commercial traveller my father did as little travelling as possible. In no time at all he had sewn up the smaller territory of the Six Counties. Rising late and after a breakfast of tea and Woodbines, he would accumulate the day's orders over the telephone. "I've got a lovely little number here, Mr. Gillespie. Only £200. No, you won't be disappointed." He was that rare thing, an Englishman accepted and trusted by Ulstermen. Handsome, charming, deft with people, he could have gone far in public life, I believe. He had enjoyed his charismatic fundraising days, but now preferred to stay at home, in retreat. I picture him chainsmoking in his dressing-gown and giving the fire a last poke before strolling to the telephone with his bundle of catalogues.

Having lived through so much by the time he was thirty, perhaps my father deserved his early partial retirement. At the age of seventeen he had enlisted in 1914, one of thousands queuing up outside Buckingham Palace. He joined the London-Scottish by mistake and went into battle wearing an unwarranted kilt. A Lady from Hell. Like so many survivors he seldom talked about his experiences, reluctant to relive the nightmare. But not long before he died, we sat up late one night and he reminisced. He had won the Military Cross for knocking out single-handed a German machine-gun post and, later, the Royal Humane Society's medal for gallantry: he had saved two nurses from drowning. By the time he was twenty he had risen to the rank of Captain, in charge of a company known as 'Longley's Babies' because many of them were not yet regular shavers. He recalled the lice, the rats, the mud, the tedium, the terror. Yes, he had bayoneted men and still dreamed about a tubby little German who "couldn't run fast enough. He turned around to face me and burst into tears." My father was nicknamed Squib in the trenches. For the rest of his life no-one ever called him Richard.

After the war he travelled through Europe as part of an anti-German propaganda mission, which he found distasteful. ("Goebbels learnt a lot from us.") He also disliked the snobbery of the officers' mess where he was dismissed as a "trench officer", his medals failing to outweigh the fact that he had not attended public school or Sandhurst. But for this he might have become a career soldier. Instead he vanished to West Africa and mined tin and gold there until he was thirty. In the photographs from Europe and Africa he is often accompanied by beautiful women. As I grew older, I noticed that he behaved most vitally in women's company, and most peacefully as well. For him a sense of unexpected bonus pervaded all the ordinary aspects of life: he could not take being alive for granted. He once showed me the gas-burns like birth-marks on his shoulder, the scars on his legs. Running away from a successful German offensive, he had been wounded by shrapnel without feeling any pain. Back in his dug-out he discovered that he had been shot through his scrotum, that the top of his penis had been severed. His children owe their existence to skilled medical orderlies. We were three further bonuses whom he enjoyed deeply and with as little fuss as possible.

III

To use a geological metaphor, my father's personality was sedimentary, my mother's volcanic. She had been born with a congenital hip malformation and walked with a severe limp. My grandmother, a beautiful Jewess called Jessica Braham, died at the age of twenty when my mother was still a baby. My Grandpa George, a man of limited sensibility, then married his housekeeper Maud who was insanely jealous of her step-child. My mother's childhood was an unrelieved misery: daily humiliations, mental and physical cruelty. My heart goes out to the little girl cowering in a corner, sobbing at the top of the dark stairs. My father told me of the first time he visited his future in-laws. Maud rushed at the young couple sitting nervously on the sofa, scrabbed her nails down my mother's face and ran out of the room screaming. When my parents had departed on their honeymoon, Maud took the wedding guests up to my mother's bedroom to show them the mess she had left it in (after working overtime the night before at her job in a record shop). My father's mother, by all accounts a saintly women, said to the embarrassed assembly, "You know the trouble with Maud? She's jealous!" Everytime I remember that story I savour the release of vengeance.

When they married, my mother was not yet twenty and my father thirty. She told me several times of their first meeting. "He was just back from Nigeria, tanned, a bit overweight but terribly dashing. I stopped to admire his red setter and he invited me to meet him in a tearoom the following week. He was something of a local hero in Clapham. Could have had any girl he wanted. Why did he choose me with my dot-and-carry walk? I still wonder. In the tearoom he said, as bold as brass, 'We're going to have wallpaper like that when we get married.'" Soon they were living in Belfast and Clapham shrank to a yearly phone-call to Grandpa George on Christmas Day, birthday cards from Auntie Daisy. I visited Daisy and two of my father's brothers, Maurice and Charlie, when I was sixteen and on holiday in London. I never met Uncle Hugh, nor my paternal grandparents (he was a journeyman carpenter, she the possessor of second sight). Because my mother's retarded brother had molested her, Grandpa George threw him out of the house. He was last heard of following the stretcher parties across No Man's Land with a sack into which he was putting bits and pieces of soldiers.

So there was no hinterland of aunts, uncles and cousins to which Wendy, Peter and I could escape and still feel at home. Perhaps because of my father's passivity, her children became the main outlet for my mother's emotions. Her moods changed unpredictably. It has taken me a long time to forgive her that atmosphere of uncertainty, its anxieties, even fears. I appreciate now that somewhere inside her intelligent humorous personality crouched the tormented child. Perhaps I was responding to this even as a boy when I would bring her sticky little bags of sweets as peace-offerings. My father sat quietly until the storm clouds passed. If this was taking too long, he would venture, "A little gin and orange, Connie?" Out of sight in the kitchen he would take a long swig of neat gin before presenting the drinks with ostentatious ceremony. "There we are, dear." Occasionally, if he realised Peter and I had been really disturbed by the climactic changes, he would say, "Your mum may walk a little funny, but she's a marvellous woman all the same." A well-meant but patronising simplification.

I remember her solving crosswords swiftly in ink. She was a first-class bridge player. My parents did not engage in any regular social intercourse except for bridge parties. Where were their close friends? My mother's good moods could be a firework display of wit and surreal invention. She would laugh for minutes at a time, her eyes watering, so that even when Peter and I were too young to understand the joke we would join in. Though her bad moods meant perhaps that the child in her was competing with us, her generosities as a mother could be bottomless. During the war she limped down many streets to buy us second-hand tricycles and other toys. Despite rationing, powdered eggs, Oxo cubes, parsnip disguised as banana, we looked forward to her carefully prepared meals. Like my father, she was depressive, and the latter part of Peter's and my childhood probably coincided with her menopause. By that time she would have been well into her forties, my father in his mid-fifties. They withdrew into themselves still further, and Wendy, a maturing teenager who at sixteen had already fallen in love with her future husband, Ernie Clegg, started to fill the emotional gaps. She became my second surrogate mother.

IV

Grandpa George was the only relative who crossed the water to visit us. He took the train to Stranraer, then the boat to Larne—an ordeal for a man in his eighties. On arrival he would claim that his journey had been "in the lap of the gods", a phrase I pretended to understand. Grandpa had been a teacher of ballroom dancing in Clapham. Top hat and tails, sequins and swirling tulle. He liked to dress up and hold centre stage, a natural master of ceremonies. His chief ambition, to be Mayor of Battersea, was never realised, despite his masonic connections (he had risen as high as Worshipful Master). I realise now that he could be vulgar and pompous, but at the time I found his Cockney accent with its genteel adjustments, his taste for polysyllables and periphrases, really exotic. A good meal was always "a highly satisfactory repast". Inclined to choke at the dinner table, he would declare, "A particle of food would appear to have lodged itself against my uvula." Every morning he would give us a full account of his "motions" (I guessed what that word meant). Laxatives, All-Bran, elastic stockings, Vic, Thermogene, long johns: these were among his obsessions. At the seaside he would roll up his trousers and rub seaweed on his white shins. "Iodine, Michael. Good for the pores." On a calm day he would lie at the water's edge and siphon the sea through his long nose. Legs astride, bending over, he would then snort out a stream of snot. "Salt water, Michael. Very good for the tubes."

Grandpa taught me cribbage, a card game not much played in Ireland. I was happy to listen to his endless monologues and fantasies as we pegged up and down the board: he needed an audience. Rickets had left him with bow-legs. "Got those riding horses. The calvary. Tipperary, 1916." Sometimes it was the Boer War (he was jealous of my father's military record). He never mentioned his retarded son, and found it impossible to accept that he had fathered a physically imperfect daughter. "A nurse dropped little Connie on the floor after she was delivered." He referred once or twice, tearfully, to Jessica Braham and seemed after all those years to be in love with her still. He also passed on to me an interest in good food and drink about which he knew a great deal. I owe to him my first taste of pheasant, hare, smoked salmon, tripe and onions, lambs' kidneys. He allowed me to sip his Guinness.

Towards the end of his life I visited Grandpa George and Maud in London. They had rented out the rest of their house and were living in the ballroom in a maze of screens and curtains. Grandpa wept then, partly because I could not stay, partly because of the pain a catheter was causing him. "The waterworks, Michael. The waterworks." Maud burst out laughing. She may have been embarrassed, but I still hate those giggles. When he died in 1958 I was the only member of our family able to attend the funeral. A few of his old cronies turned up and went to the house afterwards. "I need a whiskey," Maud said. "I've a bottle in the cabinet over there, but I'm not giving any of it to you lot." This saddened rather than shocked me, because at the crematorium her tears had made on the linoleum circles the size of half-crowns. And she had sighed again and again, "Poor George. Poor George. Poor George."

V

Being a twin meant that until I was sixteen I hardly ever slept alone. My father had painted our names in red on the cream bed-heads and covered one wall with Disney characters. The Boys' Room. We fought a lot, our differences so freely expressed that it is only recently that Peter and I have recognised how much we have in common as personalities. Beneath the tussles, tangles, power struggles an affection developed, natural, quotidian, inexpressible, so deep and lasting that to comprehend it would be a madness. I was a withdrawn watcher, Peter a rebel. If he was chastised, I would shed tears of sympathy. When he was ten Wendy and I visited Peter in hospital where he was recovering from an eye-operation. Bandages covered both his eyes, but I knew he was crying as we prepared to leave. No surge of passion or compassion in later life has quite equalled the wracking of my whole being that I experienced then. His eyes were still in bandages when he returned home. I remember reading to him at night from *The Water Babies* and *The Snow Queen* and feeling completely fulfilled—fraternal, paternal, maternal. Being a lover, a husband, a father has since enabled me to draw parallel lines only.

VI

Because of our reduced circumstances my parents could not afford to send Peter and me to one of the posher preparatory schools. (They were both old-fashioned Tories.) We attended the local Public Elementary School where, out of a large class of nearly forty pupils, we were almost the only middle-class children. Most of the others lived on "the wrong side" of the Lisburn Road. Their clothes were different from ours— woollen balaclavas, laced boots with studs in the soles. Alongside them Peter and I must have appeared chubby and well-scrubbed. I noticed at once the skinny knees and snotty noses, but most of all the accent, abrasive and raucous as a football rattle. This I soon acquired in order to make myself less unacceptable. "Len' us a mey-ek"—"Lend me a make" (a ha'penny). At home I would try to remember to ask for "a slice of cake" and not "a slice a' cey-ek", to refer to the "door" and the "floor" rather than "doo-er" and "floo-er". By the age of six or seven I was beginning to lead a double life, learning how to recreate myself twice daily.

I made friends with the other pupils and started to explore the Lisburn Road. Belfast's more prosperous citizens have usually been careful to separate themselves safely from the ghettoes of the bellicose working classes. An odd exception is the Lisburn Road which runs south from the city centre. Intermittently for about three miles workers' tiny two-up-and-two-down houses squint across the road at the drawing-rooms of dentists, doctors, solicitors: on the right, as you drive towards Lisburn gardenless shadowy streets; on the left rhododendrons and rose bushes. Belfast laid bare, an exposed artery.

I spent much of my childhood drifting from one side to the other, visiting the homes of my new friends: the lavatory outside in the yard, stairs ascending steeply as you entered, low ceilings and no elbow-room at all. My first tea at Herbie

Smith's was fried bread sprinkled with salt. Herbie came to our house and gasped when he saw the size of our back garden. For the first time I felt ashamed of our relative affluence. Our separate drawing and dining-rooms, the hall with its wooden panelling, the lavatory upstairs were all novelties to Herbie. He seemed curious rather than envious. Every corner of the home I had taken for granted was illuminated by his gaze as by wintry sunlight.

Another pupil John McCluskey was often caned for being late. He delivered papers for Younger the newsagent. If the *Belfast News-Letter* was delayed, John without complaint or explanation would be standing at 9.30 in front of the class, his hand presented to the whistling cane and then hugged under his armpit as he stumbled over schoolbags to his desk. Should I have told the teacher that he delivered papers to our house? Sometimes, as though to drown his sorrows, John would swig the blue-grey sludge from one of the small white inkwells. Every December my father gave me a half-crown as a Christmas box for the paper boy, as he called him. I never told my father that the paper boy was in my class. On the doorstep John McCluskey and I behaved like strangers and avoided each other's eyes as the half-crown changed hands. Later in class the transaction would not be mentioned.

John and Herbie shared with me their mythology which was mostly concerned with Roman Catholics. Did I know why Taigs crossed themselves? What dark practices lurked behind confession and Mass? Didn't the nuns kidnap little girls and imprison them behind the suspiciously high walls of the big convent at the top of the Ormeau Road? The Orange Order and the 'B' Specials marched through our conversations. The son of English parents, I was, at nine, less politically aware than my classmates. A photograph at home of Grandpa George lording it in his Mason's apron prompted me once to speak with snooty disparagement of the less dignified Orangemen. I was sent to Coventry until I apologised. To secure the conversion two friends smuggled me under the desk pamphlets which purported to describe Catholic atrocities from the twenties and thirties. Every page carried blurred photographs of victims who, it was claimed, had been tortured and mutilated, their brains or hearts cut out, their genitals chopped off. Forgeries? Adaptations of photographs of road accidents from forensic files? Or real victims? This vitriolic propaganda burned deep into my mind, and I perused those grim pages with the same obsessiveness that I was later to devote to *The Red Light* and nudist magazines. I craved the bond of shared fears and superstitions.

At primary school (and later at grammar school) there was little on the curriculum to suggest that we were living in Ireland: no Irish history except when it impinged on the grand parade of English monarchs; no Irish literature; no Irish art; no Irish music. When we sang in music classes we mouthed English songs. One inspector criticised our accents and forced us to sing, "Each with his bonny lawss / A dawncing on the grawss." Our teacher in Form Three, an affable man who coaxed us through the Three Rs with care and skill, became tense when for one term we were joined by a boy from Dublin—a Protestant but still a focus for our suspicions. Having flirted for a while with the unfortunate nine-year-old's political ignorance and with his own paranoia, the teacher eventually decided to confront this embodiment of menace and treachery. It was a crude question.

"Niall, who owns Belfast?"

"Dublin, sir."

"Who? Who?" This was much more than he had hoped for. "To the front of the class, boy."

"Who owns Belfast?"

"Dublin, sir." A slap in the face.

"Who told you that?" Another slap. A spittly crescendo of hatred.

"My granny, sir." More slaps. And Niall in tears.

We were invited to correct the error, to put down the rebellion. We did so and felt frightened and exhilarated.

With its dozens of little shops and the Regal Cinema where entrance to the front stalls cost threepence the Lisburn Road became my hinterland. The cinema was demolished not so long ago, and many of the shops have now been transformed into Chinese restaurants and fast food take-aways. But the rows of back-to-back houses remain, the homes of Herbie Smith, John McCluskey, Norman Hamilton, Sally Patterson, John Boland, Alan Gray, Helen Ferguson, Norma Gamble.

VII

I went on to specialise in classics at grammar school and university. Peter left home at sixteen to take up an apprenticeship. He is now Chief Engineer on a Shell tanker and lives in Newcastle-upon-Tyne. Wendy and her family live in Toronto. My father died in 1960 when I was twenty and too young to appreciate his strengths or understand his weaknesses. My mother died in April 1979. For about a year beforehand we both knew that she was going to die. I wanted to feel free to embrace her as I had embraced Lena, and agreed to call with her every day for five minutes or five hours—for as long as both of us could stand it. Over several tumultuous months we lived out her childhood and mine. She gave me X-ray pictures in which the shadowy shapes of Peter and me curl up and tangle about five months after conception. ("Tuppenny Stung for a penny bung," my father had said.) She confessed that in the early days of the pregnancy she had attempted in an amateurish way to abort us—or "it" as we then were. I registered neither shock nor pain. Somehow this knowledge made it easier for me to hug her dying lopsided body. It was like a courtship, and I accompanied her on my arm to death's door.

VIII

Since April 1979 I have been promising myself that some day I shall phone New York and talk across the Atlantic with Lena.

1985

THE EMPTY HOLES OF SPRING
Remembering Trinity and The Group

I

Trinity Days

Derek Mahon and I are both Instonians, old boys of the Royal Belfast Academical Institution. I first viewed him guiltily out of the corner of my eye in the school library. I felt guilty because the Muse had already brushed me lightly with her wing when I was sixteen, but I had ignored the invitation and allowed that side of myself to go underground. An aesthete in private, a hearty in public who briefly made it onto the 1st XV, I followed my friends in smirking knowingly when Mahon was pointed out. "Thinks he's a poet." Both aspiration and title warranted ridicule. Two years my junior, he had published amazingly accomplished verses in *School News*. In my late adolescence I did not have that kind of courage, though the publication of a few essays over the years had given me a taste for seeing my words in print.

Without having said even hello to him, I left Mahon in his sunny corner of the Inst library and headed in 1958 for Trinity College, Dublin, where my already half-hearted hold on Latin and Greek was further enfeebled by a now all-consuming desire to write poetry. I produced several splurges every day for a year or more without even realising there might be formal problems. By the time I was good enough to have some tiny lyrics accepted by the undergraduate literary magazine, *Icarus*, Mahon breezed in from Belfast to unsettle my fragile sense of myself as a 'college poet'. I had been keeping an eye on his appearances in *School News*, and was half-hoping that he would not be coming to Trinity. I remember the exact spot in Front Square where we first met at the beginning of the 1960 Michaelmas Term. "Are you Longley?" Perhaps I was expecting salutations from a fellow Instonian, even a hint of literary deference. "Can I borrow your typewriter?" He appeared rather short and very cocky.

By this time I was on the editorial board of *Icarus*. Mahon's first poem in its pages was called 'Subsidy Bungalows'—a witty portrait in shapely rhymed stanzas of his home ground, Glengormley. The voice of authority rang through every line. Michael Leahy, a philosophy student and a sophisticated stylist, a dominating presence at editorial meetings, spoke up: "This fella Mahon's good. Who is he?" And he read out a few lines. Other board members disagreed. I wanted to go along with them, but I screwed myself up to be honest and agreed that here for sure was a brilliant debut.

In my own work I was homing in with radar-accuracy on the weaknesses of good poets, combining the tweeness of E.E. Cummings, for instance, with the portentousness of Wallace Stevens:

I see in your eyes words big as thunder
On your silent lips the small sound of roses ...

That's how I began a piece called 'Love Poem'—pretty wan and effete compared to Mahon's 'Love Poem' (in the same issue of *Icarus*) with its élan and elemental propulsion:

Holding her in my arm I feel quite clearly
The trickle of muscles where the sea wind,
Over the stones and bones love crowns with cockles,
Whistles and seems to indicate the moon,
Whose ancient rule neap love and spring love tells.

Nerves sing and sing that the thin water
Is drawn in sand, the chill sea disinherits
Of all unfathomable movements his offspring,—
Young anemones opening in their bed,
The still cancer lifting ...

Echoes of Hart Crane, Robert Graves and Dylan Thomas do not diminish the originality of this writing. Mahon's uncollected juvenilia is finer than the life's work of many poets. As precociously assured as early Auden, it is matched in English only by the several poems of Keith Douglas and the few by Geoffrey Hill which each composed before he was twenty. I felt overwhelmed and wanted to withdraw to a safe distance. But poets, because they should never completely grow up, must continually come of age. I began to come of age—or came of age for the first time—when I decided to embrace the pain of friendship with a younger poet who seemed already to have arrived while I was just setting out.

In 'River & Fountain', the quatercentenary poem I wrote for my old college more than thirty years later, I describe life in rooms as "village of minds, poetry's townland":

Top of the staircase, Number Sixteen in Botany Bay,
Slum-dwellers, we survived gas-rings that popped, slop-
Buckets in the bedrooms, changeable 'wives', and toasted
Doughy doorsteps, Freshmen turning into Sophisters
In front of the higgledy flames: our still-life, crusts
And buttery books, the half-empty marmalade jar.

Mahon did turn up there to borrow my typewriter. Our long friendship got under way with that transaction and an opening conversation about punctuation. The eighth line of 'Love Poem', above, reveals an already elegant deployer of the wee marks. Mahon claimed that it was one of his ambitions to end a line with three dots, a bracket and a dash [...)—]. I can't recall if he has yet pulled off this dizzy feat.

Reading Classics, even in half-hearted fashion, meant that I wasn't as well-read as I should have been in English literature. It was a joy to go on a guided tour of poetry with a well-informed companion. On my Dansette record player I provided high-class background music from LPs as thick and heavy as dinner plates—some jazz but mainly Sibelius, Brahms, Stravinsky. Later Mahon wrote a lovely poem about our shared experience and differing attitudes, 'Brahms Trio', which he never collected:

We wrestled with your temperamental turntable,
Its pilot light and roving arm—
I scarcely noticed at the time
What an impression that fluffy needle made.

In the poem's mythology I chose to spend my "late nights listening to the Symphonies" while the authorial 'I' was "drawn on by raw material noise". I still have by heart three lines from the closing stanza:

I hear each instrument come in,
Piano, cello, violin,
And recognise this as my favourite sound ...

We inhaled with our untipped Sweet Afton cigarettes MacNeice, Crane, Dylan Thomas, Yeats, Larkin, Lawrence,

Graves, Ted Hughes, Stevens, Cummings, Richard Wilbur, Robert Lowell, as well as Rimbaud, Baudelaire, Brecht, Rilke—higgledepiggledy, in any order. We scanned the journals and newspapers for poems written yesterday. When Larkin's 'The Whitsun Weddings' first appeared in *Encounter*, Mahon steered me past the documentary details, which as an aspiring lyricist I found irritating, to the poem's resonant, transcendental moments. He introduced me to George Herbert who thrilled me as though he were a brilliant contemporary published that very week by the Dolmen Press. Herbert, thanks to Mahon, is a beneficent influence in my first collection and provides the stanzaic templates for two of its more ambitious poems.

In the early sixties the best known 'college poets' were Brendan Kennelly and Rudi Holzapfel who, first out of the traps by a long way, had already published by 1963 four shared collections. Kennelly, a few years my senior, had been generous, welcoming, encouraging. As assistant editor and then as editor of *Icarus* he had accepted several of my juvenilia at just the right time in my slow development. He and Holzapfel gave a reading to the College's Laurentian Society (a Catholic outfit) which Mahon and I attended. The small room was packed. Towards the end of the evening we were taken aback when Kennelly, with a twinkle, introduced us to the audience and invited us to read a poem or two. I rushed back to my rooms and grabbed my folder. I was too overwhelmed to register Mahon's performance, but I remember my heart thumping as I read my own words aloud to an audience for the first time. My poem was called 'The Threshold Shore', and Deborah de Vere White came up to me afterwards to say that she had enjoyed it. We stagger through such occasions without realising their significance. It pleases me now that Kennelly was our godfather at that initiation.

We smoked and drank too much. If not in Number Sixteen, our seminars were held in O'Neill's Bar, Suffolk Street. From time to time we breakfasted on pints. Mahon embodied for me the spirit of Pan or Puck when he played the tin whistle in Victor Blease's rooms and walked up and down the furniture as though weightless. We laughed a lot. A need to undermine Northern Irish middle-class respectability seemed to be at the core of our humour. Although pieties of any kind were fit targets, a posh Cherryvalley accent which caricatured the wobbly vowel-sounds of the more complacent brands of Unionism invariably focused our hilarity. But these were fulfilling rather than happy times. Our friendship and our abilities were often stretched as far as they could go. I admired Mahon's disenchanted vision, but was less attracted than he to the role of *poète maudit*. Nevertheless, when I suffered a brainstorm and walked out of my finals, it was Mahon who tracked me down to Amiens Street station (as it then was) and in tones of unwonted avuncular concern tried to talk some sense into my head.

The following year we shared a malodorous basement flat in Merrion Square. We hoped that microbes in the dregs would devour each other and in cannibalistic frenzy render clean our extensive collection of milk bottles. We put used bed-linen and dirty clothes back in drawers where they might refresh themselves according to the principles of the septic tank. The persistent presence of a toothless, garrulous concierge ever eager to share with us her dental and gynaecological problems helped to make the scene a combination of Beckett and O'Casey. In order to finance myself I worked for a pittance as a miserably ineffective Latin master at a school in Blackrock. Unable to maintain order, exhausted by the end of the day, I somehow managed to keep my Classics afloat for a second attempt at moderatorship. All the while I was responding to Mahon's poetic challenge. I returned to our shadowy basement after the Easter break to find the fireplace behind the electric fire stuffed with screwed-up balls of paper, the draughts of 'Legacies', his Villon translation. This inspired me to concentrate my dwindling energies on a version of Propertius's great 'Cornelia' elegy in rhymed ten-line stanzas. Mahon's verve and edginess helped to keep me sane.

Terence de Vere White started to publish our verse in the *Irish Times* (the first poem I ever sold: £5 for 'The Flying Fish'). The *Dublin Magazine* took over from *Icarus* as our main outlet. Since 1960 I had been courting Edna Broderick, the daughter of the Professor of Pure Mathematics and, unlike me, a real scholar. She had contributed to *Icarus* essays on Cummings and Wilbur, and had reviewed our own efforts favourably in *Trinity News*—enough to make her our friend for life! After a couple of detours I followed her to Belfast where she had been appointed lecturer in English at Queen's University. Mahon was the dapper best man at our wedding the day before New Year's Eve 1964. By that time he had brought Eavan Boland up to Belfast to meet us, and we had been getting to know Seamus Heaney and his future wife, Marie Devlin. It was a relief as well as an excitement to meet others for whom poetry meant everything, and to sense the "village of minds, poetry's townland" extending infinitely.

1994

II

The Group

Some people seem to think that Derek Mahon, James Simmons, Seamus Heaney and I were the discoveries of Philip Hobsbaum, and that we served our apprenticeships together at the sessions of The Group. I never saw Simmons at a Group meeting, and Mahon was present only once or twice as a kind of outside observer when he happened to be back in Belfast and staying with me. Initially I had no desire to attend, but Hobsbaum who was a colleague of my fiancée's invited us both along. The Group was a going concern by then: I can in no way be seen as a founding member.

From the beginning Hobsbaum made it clear that his stars were Seamus Heaney and Stewart Parker, who was teaching in the States at this time. Hobsbaum's aesthetic demanded gritty particularity, an unrhetorical utterance. Heaney's work fitted the bill especially well: at the second or third meeting which I attended a sheet of his poems was discussed—'Digging' and 'Death of a Naturalist' (it was called 'End of a Naturalist' then).

By this time I was beginning to enjoy what was for me as a lapsed Classicist a new experience—practical criticism. But I didn't much care for The Group aesthetic or, to be honest, the average poem which won approval. I believed that poetry should be polished, metrical and rhymed; olique rather than head-on; imagistic and symbolic rather than rawly factual; rhetorical rather than documentary. I felt like a Paleface among a tribe of Redskins. Although I have since modified my ideas, I still think that despite the rigours of practical criticism and the kitchen heat of the discussions, many Group poems tended to be underdone.

There was a short story by Hugh Bredin which I liked— my first meeting, so as far as I can remember. I wonder why he hasn't continued writing fiction. Arthur Terry's fine translations from the Spanish and Catalan featured regularly: the best-read man I have ever met. I think that he in particular found The Group a useful stimulus, as did Norman Dugdale, a top civil servant who had been writing poetry secretly for years. And then there was Jack Pakenham, a painter who rather disapproved of what everyone else was producing, and who backed up his often outspoken criticism with his own free-wheeling surrealist verse. Hobsbaum had a radar capacity for spotting any pen as soon as it touched paper.

When my turn came I was expecting sharp criticism, but was rather surprised by the ferocity of Hobsbaum's attack and the incomprehension which my work seemed to inspire in everyone else. Just before Hobsbaum left Belfast for Glasgow he admitted that I was really quite good, but up until then I had been encouraged to think of myself as a degenerate sophisticate. This merely confirmed me in my ways—in fact I used to look forward masochistically to the seasonal maulings. I can honestly say that I did not alter one semi-colon as the result of Group discussion. Which sounds smug: perhaps I should add that as undergraduate poets at Trinity College, Derek Mahon and I had been tough on each other—more hurtful than The Group ever was. In any case I realised that I could count on an undercurrent of support from Harry Chambers, Arthur Terry, Michael Allen, Seamus Heaney and the late John Harvey who was a marvellous Professor of English for a tragically brief period. (Chambers and Allen were eventually purged, cast out from the magic circle.)

Friendship with these people and with Hobsbaum remains for me the most important legacy of The Group. The poetry would have happened anyway. Hobsbaum brought some of us together and generated an atmosphere of controversy and excitement. He committed himself to Belfast and the writers here with great energy and generosity, and when he left there was really no reason for The Group to continue.

1976

BLACKTHORN & BONSAI
or, A Little Brief Authority

... man, proud man,
Dress'd in a little brief authority,—
Most ignorant of what he's most assured ...

—Measure for Measure

I

I am a founder member of the Cultural Traditions Group which came together nearly four years ago with the aim of encouraging acceptance and understanding of cultural diversity in Northern Ireland. We went public the following year by holding a conference called *Varieties of Irishness*. The distinguished Irish historian Roy Foster gave the keynote lecture at the end of which he referred to a poetry reading tour undertaken by John Hewitt and John Montague away back in November 1970. Foster talked of Hewitt "... who articulated that quintessential combination of Protestant scepticism and commitment, linked with a sense of place that was absolutely Irish." He went on to say that "Hewitt's poetry tour with John Montague in 1970, *The Planter and the Gael*, was a landmark affirmation of creative cultural diversity." *The Planter and the Gael* was the first event which I organised for the Arts Council of Northern Ireland. The booklet which accompanied the tour carried this rubric: "In the selection of his poems each poet explores his experience of Ulster, the background in which he grew up and the tradition which has shaped his work. The two bodies of work complement each other and provide illuminating insight into the cultural complexities of the Province."

In this lecture I shall tell the story of my twenty-one years as an arts administrator and bureaucrat—from 1970 and *The Planter and the Gael* to the late eighties/early nineties and my involvement with the Cultural Traditions movement—two decades in which momentous and often terrible things have happened in Ulster, in Ireland. As I picked my way through the mine-field, I operated intuitively rather than intellectually.

So I shall be talking about what happened. Events brought my beliefs to the surface, and confirmed or changed my ideas.

II

It was often a struggle to secure modest budgets for disciplines which were not represented by powerful lobbies, a struggle against vested interests. The 'blackthorn' of my title represents indigenous talent (the writers and traditional musicians who—along with some painters—are the main reason why we enjoy a cultural reputation abroad. They are also, of course, sources of energy at home). The 'bonsai' stands for money-devouring activities such as orchestral music and opera which in their Irish manifestations make comparatively little impact on the world stage. The analogy crumbles a bit when we realise that the Japanese, unlike our own cultural panjandrums, intend their little trees to remain little. I was never opposed to orchestral music or opera. How could anyone be? My criticisms were directed at the quality of decision-making. Along with a few others I argued for a sense of proportion and fair play.

In the mid-eighties, for instance, the government gave the council some much-needed additional finance. Called the Special Initiative Fund, this looked like a challenge to try something new and anticipated the provision some years later for the Cultural Traditions programme. Before the staff could draw breath, we learned that a large portion of the fund had already been allocated to the Ulster Orchestra—without any discussion. In expressing caution about this pre-emptive strike we merely wanted the case for the orchestra's enlargement to be considered in the context of the council's over-all programme and weighed in the same set of scales as other proposals. In order to encourage open discussion we prepared against the clock detailed papers for the next meeting of the board. We were surprised and disappointed when the chairman of the day devoted most of the available time to leading a well-attended meeting line by line through the foreword to that year's annual report—an effective filibuster; a costly method of sub-editing. Stalled at the green light, we watched juggernauts crash the red.

In my address to a joint meeting of the two Irish Arts Councils at the Ulster Folk Museum in 1983 I imagined the ghosts of present administrators being interrogated by their great-great-grandchildren: "Well, thank you for buttressing the reputations of Mozart and Beethoven, but what did you do to promote the great singing of Eddie Butcher and Sarah Makem, the virtuoso fiddling of Johnny Doherty? In the 1980s there was an important dramatic movement in Belfast that produced many interesting urban working-class plays. What did you do to make it possible for these talents to work in and illuminate the back streets from which they emerged?"

I went on to suggest that the imbalance between support for the performing arts and support for the creators pointed to other imbalances. In the sphere of arts administration there was a danger of administration outweighing the arts. For instance, every year the council organises a Regional Conference for local art committee members and town councillors. Why, I asked, should there not take place every five years or so a conference for artists? There was also a class imbalance. In relation to the size of its middle class Belfast has the largest working class in Europe. The price alone of many council events puts them out of reach. The people ideally suited to bring the arts to what we termed 'deprived areas' were the local artists. These ideas suggested a third imbalance—that between 'mail-order culture' and the nurturing of indigenous talent. There were, for example, financial reasons why the Grand Opera House in Belfast should import tinsel; but it seemed shortsighted to import so much tinsel when we were sitting on a goldmine which was still relatively underexploited. Ulster no longer merited the playwright Sam Thompson's dismissal—"a cultural Siberia". In as much as creative imaginations could now get by there, the province had become less provincial. Releasing original talents into the community should be the council's profoundest involvement. The response to my aria was muted.

Over the years I would from time to time ask two simple questions. How much of our programme will posterity thank us for? How much of what we are doing differentiates us from Bolton or Wolverhampton? In short, "where there is no vision, the people perish." I was pleased to find a spiritual ally in the great geographer Estyn Evans who had written in *Ulster: The Common Ground*: "Certain cultural traits persist and can be related in one way or another to a pastoral heritage." He went on to suggest that "in the arts, for instance, the natural thing for the Irish is not the communal effort of expensive orchestral music but the lone fiddler."

My job was often fulfilling, and sometimes funny. *The Planter and the Gael* poetry-reading tour provided me with a lasting image. My old friend and late colleague Paul Clarke was then the Arts Council's Promotions Officer. At the last moment he decided on some nifty presentational improvements—among them throne-like seats for our two bards. The varnish had not dried out in time for the opening night, so that when the always dignified John Hewitt rose to recite his first poem, there was a loud ripping noise. In the Arts Council I occasionally sensed a similar backwards tug as I prepared to rise.

There are five Arts Councils on the archipelago: one in Belfast, one in Dublin and, across the water, the Scottish and Welsh Arts Councils which are funded by the fifth and largest body, the Arts Council of Great Britain. This began its days after the last war as a morale-booster with the unbalanced title of Council for the Encouragement of Music and the Arts (CEMA). A Northern Irish model followed several years later. It was beginning to make up for lost time, when the eruption of civic violence in the late sixties and early seventies caused what Kenneth Jamison, the Council's Director for more than twenty years, has rather euphemistically called "a protracted spasm of social paralysis". From this paralysis there are—as audience statistics demonstrate—remissions. The Council is funded by the Northern Ireland Office through the Department of Education, and the sum allocated to it this year is in the region of £6,000,000. Its objects are to improve the practice and appreciation of the arts and to increase their accessibility to the people of Northern Ireland.

III

At the invitation of its Director, Kenneth Jamison, I joined the Council in 1970 as a temporary Exhibitions Officer. (I had been reviewing local art exhibitions for the *Irish Times*; and I had got to know the Director as the result of *Room to Rhyme*, a touring entertainment organised by him in 1968 and featuring songs from David Hammond and poems read by Seamus Heaney and myself.) A few years before my arrival the Board had decreed that because it was practised by amateurs, literature did not come within its remit (so much for part-time scribblers like T.S. Eliot, bank clerk and publisher, and for those in insurance or medicine like Wallace Stevens and William Carlos Williams). I was encouraged to create some kind of a role for myself. In my first year, as well as hanging pictures and lecturing about them, I edited *Causeway*, a comprehensive survey of the arts in Ulster, and an anthology of poetry written by children called *Under the Moon, Over the Stars*; and I initiated the programme for literature with a budget of £3000. Those earliest grants included £143 for the *Honest Ulsterman* magazine; £50 each for poetry pamphlets by Frank Ormsby and Ciaran Carson; £150 for *Soundings*, a magazine edited by Seamus Heaney; £1000 for the Blackstaff Press and six titles by, among others, Sam Hanna Bell, James Simmons and Stewart Parker; and £800 for the Dublin publishing house of Gill & Macmillan to bring out pioneering critical studies by two academics from Northern Ireland who were already registering the new creative buzz: *Forces and Themes in Ulster Fiction* by John Wilson Foster and *Northern Voices: Poets from Ulster* by Terence Brown.

Despite my ignorance, I initiated in 1972/73, with a tiny budget, a programme for what we eventually christened the traditional arts. One of the first people I contacted was Estyn Evans. I invited him to select the images and prepare a commentary for a book of R.J. Welch's photographs of Ireland and Irish life at the end of the last century. Published some time later by Blackstaff Press, *Ireland's Eye* heralded the revival of interest in our pioneer photographers as readily assimilable interpreters of our common past. In his introduction Evans writes about the Belfast Naturalists' Field Club of which Welch was a leading member: "The Field Club was non-sectarian, and it seems to have attracted men of good will who deplored the political and sectarian fragmentation that disfigured the face of Belfast."

In 1972 John Hewitt retired from his job as Art Director of the Herbert Art Gallery and Museum in Coventry, and returned after a fifteen year exile to Belfast and his remarkably productive Indian summer. In his introduction to *Ireland's Eye* Estyn Evans speculates: "It would be interesting to trace the relationship between the field club movement and another phenomenon which was more directly a cultural by-product of the textile industry in Ulster. Throughout the province, as John Hewitt has shown in his book *Rhyming Weavers*, the weaving areas produced many poets, especially in the first half of the nineteenth century, some of them showing considerable talent." Like a kestrel hovering above a tiny field, Evans wonders about "the links between the work involved in handling different kinds of natural fibres and regional patterns of cultural expression."

The mutual awareness of Evans and Hewitt dated from the 1940s when the philosophy of regionalism had been vigorously debated. They inspired my thinking, and gave me a sense of continuity. Thanks to them, the programmes for literature and the traditional arts began to overlap and provide shelter for modest but timely explorations. Hewitt had already written my script: "Out of that loyalty to our own place, rooted in honest history, in familiar folk-ways and knowledge, phrased in our own dialect, there should emerge a culture and an attitude individual and distinctive, a fine contribution to the European inheritance and no mere echo of the thought and imagination of another land."

The first traditional arts committee included real experts like Sean O Baoill, the collector of songs and Ogam's obsessive interpreter; the singer David Hammond; George Thompson of the Folk Museum; Brendan Adams who poured over dialect maps during meetings; scholars such as Deirdre Flanagan, Gerry Stockman, Rodney Green; Maurice Hayes who much later was to become the Northern Irish Ombudsman and the Chairman of the Cultural Traditions Group; Drew Donaldson who rode a big old-fashioned tricycle down the Malone Road to Methody where he taught Irish until, for want of customers, he retired, a disappointed pioneer of cultural pluralism. On the literature committee John Hewitt spoke infrequently but always with such weight few would contradict him. After meetings it was a treat to take the likes of him and Jimmy Vitty of the Linen Hall Library to the Botanic Inn for a pint or two. My education was proceeding apace.

Hierarchies are obsessed with titles. For my last nine years I was designated the Combined Arts Director. Although I oversaw Traditional Arts, Young Arts and Community Arts, colleagues now ran these programmes, and my own speciality remained literature. The central plank of this programme is, of course, publication, the printed word. Much of any arts organisation's activity resembles a tidal wave which leaves behind little or no residue. One of the pleasures of a literary post is the accumulation over the years of desirable objects with an indefinite shelf-life. The objectives define themselves: to provide publishing outlets for local authors; to facilitate the continuing existence of local publishing houses; to make available to the local community and to readers elsewhere the best of contemporary Ulster writing; to keep in print distinguished literature from the recent past; and to represent our generation to itself, the world at large, and to posterity. It was particulary exciting to be involved with the development of the Blackstaff Press, for instance. Regional in its origins and focus, this small publishing house makes Ulster (and other) voices audible around the world.

Magazines and journals which publish Irish writers and reflect the cultural life of the province (and island) are also helped along financially. The idea is to provide an outlet for young, up-and-coming authors as well as established talents; to keep the bibliographical tally up to date; and to encourage good criticism and a lively critical climate. T.S. Eliot remarked that the cultural health of a community could be judged by the liveliness or otherwise of its magazine tradition. I find some reassurance in the continuing vigour of established magazines and the emergence of new ones. An old warhorse like the *Honest Ulsterman* is known far beyond Northern Ireland. Newcomers like *Rhinoceros* provide an alternative platform, especially for young mavericks. Local writers and writing are welcomed by the political journal *Fortnight*, the back part—the cultural pages—of which I supported, despite some official pressure caused, no doubt, by the editorial policy of opening its pages to all points of view.

It is also a good idea to introduce writers to their public, to provide opportunities for the community to meet and listen to 'living writers'. An author's physical voice does influence the way he or she writes. Despite Caxton and Derrida literature still takes shape in the mouth and finds its resting place in the ear. Visitors such as Robert Lowell, Hugh

MacDiarmid, Angela Carter, Miroslav Holub, Liz Lochhead, Ian McEwan, Marin Sorescu, Tony Harrison, Joseph Brodsky, Douglas Dunn, James Fenton, Andrei Voznesensky have helped us to avoid literary inbreeding and cultural insularity. Most of the generals and field marshals of what Patrick Kavanagh humorously referred to as Ireland's "standing army" of writers have performed for us. *The Planter and the Gael* wasn't the only poetry-reading tour. *Out of the Blue* featured James Simmons and Paul Muldoon; *In their Element* Derek Mahon and Seamus Heaney. And we tried combining poetry and jazz in *Take It Away*.

Around the province audiences for these promotions were usually disappointingly small. In any case, I did not consider such tours a priority, and preferred to use limited funds to engage the community in more lasting ways. Two writer-in-residence posts at Queen's University and the University of Ulster have allowed the embryo writer to discuss his or her work with established practitioners, who, in turn, have enjoyed more time in which to create. Recently the council established a third post—that of Writer-in-Residence in the Irish language—shared between the two universities. So far as I know, there is no equivalent position elsewhere on the archipelago.

I often expressed the hope that the principles of these residencies might be extended into the community. This dream came true towards the end of my bureaucratic career when four young artists—Glenn Patterson, the novelist; Rita Duffy, the artist; Desi Wilkinson, the traditional flute-player and the photographer James Maginn—were employed by the council to work through schools and colleges, community centres, museums, libraries and local history groups. I gave this scheme the extrovert title *Outlook*, and in the explanatory brochure wrote: "The Arts Council believes that the regular interaction between artist and community will provide points of growth, new sources of creative energy, opportunities for communal self-expression, self-definition and self-expression." This, more or less, is what the brilliant quartet achieved.

This rubric and the three snatches of poetry which I slipped into the *Outlook* brochure suggest not only what I hoped the literature and traditional arts programmes might achieve, but also obstacles and disappointments. The first snippet comes from Louis MacNeice's 'Autumn Journal', Canto XVI which is about Ireland:

... one feels that here at least one can
Do local work which is not at the world's mercy
And that on this tiny stage with luck a man
Might see the end of one particular action.

The second is the ending of Patrick Kavanagh's 'Epic' which measures the Munich crisis against a local territorial squabble:

... I inclined
To lose my faith in Ballyrush and Gortin
Till Homer's ghost came whispering to my mind.
He said: I made the Iliad from such
A local row. Gods make their own importance.

Yeats's 'The Fisherman' provides the third quotation:

All day I'd looked in the face

What I had hoped 'twould be
To write for my own race
And the reality.

IV

There was a literary tinge and, in retrospect, a significant symmetry to the very first grants which I made in 1972 from the new traditional arts budget—one for *Rhyming Weavers*, John Hewitt's study of the Ulster-Scots vernacular poets of Down and Antrim; and another for a study by Tomas O Fiach—later the Cardinal—of the 18th century South Armagh Gaelic poet Art MacCooey. The experience of starting up the literature programme provided templates for the traditional arts. The same principles evolved in much the same way—except that arts administration was to become a much bumpier ride.

I knew very little about Irish music. The "wise and simple man" who opened doors and helped me to organise the first concerts and tours was a hard-drinking carpenter called Brian O'Donnell who hailed from Killybegs in Donegal but lived in the Lower Ormeau area of Belfast. He knew everyone there was to know in the world of Irish music. I revered his deep love of the tradition, and learned a lot—even from his erratic, often wild behaviour. We put on our first concert in Belfast's Civic Arts Theatre. This was seen by many as an event of symbolic importance: an organisation like the Arts Council was at last taking traditional music seriously. One of the most exciting moments of my life came when I saw the customers queueing around the block to get in. The evening acquired further symbolism. Brian, the soul of the entertainment, got so under the weather that the proprietor of the theatre, Hibby Wilmot, would not let him in. I had to decide between hearing the concert or attending to Brian's dignity. I chose the latter.

In the early seventies the North was contorted by spiralling sequences of tit-for-tat murders. These were bleak, anxious times to be touring with traditional Irish musicians. But it was crucial to challenge those who would appropriate the music for political ends and those who would excoriate it as alien and even threatening. Nor did we see the point of preaching—playing—to the converted all of the time. There had recently been an IRA atrocity in one of the country towns—mainly Protestant—where we were to play. I took the musicians into the function room of the pub which had been booked for the night. The owner of the pub said, "My bar will be blown up unless you begin or end the concert with 'The Queen'." I replied, "I have never heard 'The Queen' played on the Irish pipes!" But it was a serious impasse; and there was menace in the air. A brain-wave. "Is there a Jimmy-Shand-type accordion-player in the town?" we asked. David Hammond, the MC for the night, had a vague memory that there was such a musician in the vicinity. He might end our concert with some Scottish dance music—and then 'The Queen'. Our musical saviour turned up, and I offered him a fee. The concert proceeded with the audience talking loudly and insultingly all the way through. The gents' toilet was at the side of the small stage. Large tattooed figures lumbered backwards and forwards glaring at the musicians. David Hammond sang every Scottish song in his repertoire. The audience at last quietened for the local box-player who performed several Scottish melodies. By the time he got round to 'The Queen' we had skedaddled. The fingers and thumbs—the lives even—of the musicians had been in danger. This was not running away.

On another occasion, at the request of the UDA, we put on a small concert of Irish music in their headquarters in East Belfast. More than a polite interest was shown in the performances. Our hosts really wanted to find out why one side seemed to have most of the good tunes. We told them about great Protestant interpreters of Irish music like the singers Joe Holmes and Len Graham, the dulcimer-player John Rea of Glenarm. There was much more to their own tradition than Orange ballads, just as Nationalist ballads were only a small part of Irish music. A witty colleague who was present remarked that the faces of the musicians as they entered the UDA building put him in mind of "Egyptologists descending into a tomb." Perhaps there should be more ventures of this kind which are bold and hare-brained enough to be— literally—disarming. I was later to get involved with the Royal Scottish Pipe Band Association and gave support to their educational programme for over a decade, up to the point where they have now started classes in *Piobaireachd*. Among young players it is now fashionable to play Irish music. Last year at the championships in Inverness the top prize was won by an Ulster piper playing an Irish tune on the Scottish pipes.

Because Brian was fond of her, I booked for the second tour Maggie Barry who billed herself as 'The Singing Gypsy Woman'. I ended up loving her vast, untameable personality. Even when Maggie was singing an old chestnut like 'When Irish Eyes Are Smiling', there was something authentic about her. In Armagh I realised that the Protestant Primate,

George Simms, was sitting in the front row. I said to Maggie who was getting raunchier as the week proceeded: "Maggie, you'll never guess who's in the front row: George Simms the Protestant Primate of All Ireland!" That's all I said, I wasn't going to control her. I could not have done so no matter how hard I tried. Maggie came out and started to tune her banjo. Although she played only the one string, she liked to make a big fuss about tuning it. "I can't get this damned thing tuned at all," she exclaimed; and then with an enormous wink in the direction of the Protestant Primate: "The frets are wet and sticky, but sure isn't that me all over!" Afterwards George Simms came up to me and said, "I enjoyed the evening so much. Irish music reminds me of the intricacies of the *Book of Kells*."

For me these are parables rather than anecdotes—ways of explaining conversion and spiritual growth. Once I trailed around Donegal with Brian O'Donnell in search of the great Johnny Doherty who, although he was well into his seventies, was still on the road. Even in old age he preferred the life of the itinerant musician. He was a fiddler of consummate artistry, a genius. After a couple of days we tracked him down to a little pub where he was playing for balls of malt. Most of the small gathering chattered through his soaring music. Brian and I sat down quietly behind him. He must have registered us as an oasis of silence and concentration. When he had finished his first set he turned round slowly and nodded towards us in a dignified fashion. As a bureaucrat I tried to make sure that the least we gave to traditional musicians was an oasis of this kind of respect. I dedicated my *Poems 1963–1983* to the memory of Brian O'Donnell and another dear friend, the magistrate Martin McBirney. He and

Judge Rory Conaghan were murdered by the IRA in September 1974. On my way to Brian O'Donnell's house in Cooke Street I passed a ghastly and inaccurate graffito: "The Two Judges Ha! Ha! Ha!"

Ciaran Carson is now the custodian of literature and the traditional arts whose interconnection his own poetry—attentive to the rhythms of musician and *seanachie*—proclaims. He "looks into the future through the eyes of the past". As readers of his sparkling *Pocket Guide to Irish Music* will appreciate, his authoritative voice rings out most clearly in the dialogue between authenticity and renovation. There is an Irish proverb that "tradition is stronger than learning". Carson believes that in many cases tradition has to be recovered by learning—by personal contact, by a sensitive use of the comparatively new technology of the video and tape-recorder. He emphasises the mutual agreement of traditional music-making and its social context. "Even the most apparently informal session," he says, "is governed by a complex set of implicit rules in which conversation, singing, playing and dancing are an expression of a wider community." The grandiose title of Combined Arts Director has been bestowed on John Morrow, a wise and hilarious man, a comic author of brilliance, a humane administrator. No one's ear is more acutely tuned to the culture of his place.

Here are two statistics. With the exception of *Among Our Own*, a gala evening of readings compiled by John Hewitt and me for the 1977 Belfast Festival (it nearly filled the Whitla Hall), neither the director nor the four chairmen who served the Arts Council while I worked for it (a period of twenty-one years) attended any of the events I had funded or organised in the areas of literature and traditional music. It took me eighteen years to hoist the budget for literature up to £100,000. The budget for dance got there in eighteen months, or thereabouts.

V

About a year ago I was invited to read my poems to a group of civil servants and businessmen who were being prepared for top jobs. They had been through several taxing days in what appeared to be a series of initiation rites for the early middle-aged, a preparation for the upper reaches of the greasy pole. I was to provide the light relief. Half way through dessert I looked around at the grey suits and decided that an after-dinner session of undiluted poetry might interfere with digestion. I felt a desire to disperse the fog of managerial jargon that wafted from some of the tables. Since the theme of the course was leadership, I opened up by talking about good leadership, and gave them the best example I could think of from history (Christ washing the feet of the disciples, no less) and from the world of the arts.

Lawrence Gilliam was head of the BBC's Features Department. He employed formidable talents like Dylan Thomas, W. R. Rodgers, Henry Reed and Louis MacNeice. When the BBC needs to celebrate some anniversary or other by opening its archive, programmes from the Gilliam stable are among the few that do not date. He knew his own limitations and rejoiced in the strengths of others. Lawrence Gilliam led a brilliant department by not leading it. Gifted in his own way, he also had the moral sense and qualities of imagination to realise that he could hardly be Louis MacNeice's leader. No. He was Louis MacNeice's minder, protecting him from bureaucracy, providing him with budgets, sending him to places like India (where MacNeice covered Independence), turning a blind eye to the poet's trips to Ireland which were ostensibly reconnoitres but which almost invariably coincided with rugby internationals at Ravenhill or Lansdowne Road.

In 1945 MacNeice was exhausted. He had written and produced seventy programmes in four years. He came to Ireland to recuperate and to decide whether or not he would return to his job. "Tell them I'll take three months off—without pay," he wrote to Gilliam. "Tell them I'm an artist." Gilliam covered up for him so successfully that MacNeice enjoyed a full year's leave of absence—with pay. But his "one year off" affected broadcasting in Northern Ireland for the next twenty years and more. MacNeice made contact with W.R. Rodgers, Sam Hanna Bell and John Boyd, and brought them into broadcasting. And he returned himself with, in his pocket, *The Dark Tower*, the finest feature ever put out over the airwaves by the Third Programme. Lawrence Gilliam lived and worked according to Albert Camus' principle—"If you lead I shall not follow; if you follow I shall not lead". His career demonstrates that it is possible for an arts organisation to be arts-led, and that choosing the right people is the managerial skill that counts for most in the end.

When I proposed a modest increase in the lilliputian budget for artists' bursaries, I was invited to write a paper on awards and present it to the board. Which I did. I was then asked to present my paper to each of the advisory committees and re-submit it to the board along with a summary of their responses. Which I did. All of this took an age. Eventually nothing whatsoever happened. I secured no extra money for artists. Indeed, the system of pooled awards for all the disciplines which I had administered for several years was dismantled while I was away on sabbatical. At the time, with little or no debate at all, large deficits were being incurred for glamorous imported productions in the Grand Opera House, and then transformed retrospectively into 'Special Grants'. For four nights of Rimsky-Korsakov's *The Golden Cockerel* the deficit was £80,000—that is £20,000 per night. The annual budget for the traditional arts was then £20,000.

A few years ago I was anxious that I was going to be overspent in my literature budget. So I heard with relief that since the writer-in-residence at the University of Ulster happened to be a playwright—Martin Lynch—the post would be financed out of the budget for drama and dance. Later I learned of plans to transform the writer-in-residence into a dancer-in-residence. This was crazy logic. I cared deeply about the writer-in-residence posts, and feared that my little tapestry might unravel without this strand. When I objected, I was told that the deliberations of the drama committee were none of my business. It took energy-sapping arguments and a volley of memos to win back this position for writers. (The first writer-in-residence at Queen's had been John Hewitt; and at the University of Ulster, Derek Mahon.)

In a letter to John Quinn W.B. Yeats writes: "It is wonderful the amount of toil and intrigue one goes through to accomplish anything in Ireland. Intelligence has no organisation whilst stupidy always has." Manipulators are the blight of bureaucracy. Governed by short-term political advantage, time-servers, they do not concern themselves with—in Yeats's phrase—gradual time's last gifts. If you take them on, you tangle with a tar-baby and end up as besmirched as what you are fighting. When an organisation degenerates, its housestyle becomes furtive, deceptive, manipulative. The old anarchist slogan may indeed come true: "Government is chaos". Institutions like individuals can go off the rails. When they do, a huge effort is required to take even a few small rational steps.

VI

The dislikeable aspects of bureaucratic life combined spectacularly just over a year ago. I know what happened, but not precisely how and why. What am I about to describe? vindictiveness? the limitations and complacencies of the provincial mind? unconscious sectarianism? the freemasonry of the mediocre? simple ineptitude? all or some or none or one of these? Was this an eerie repetition of the *cause célèbre* of 1953 when after twenty-three years working for the Belfast Museum and Art Gallery John Hewitt was cruelly denied the directorship through backroom manoeuvring and for no reason other than what some officials considered his political unsuitability? This removed from the centre of things at a crucial time in our history one of the most distinguished living Ulstermen. Hewitt has described his emotions as he crossed the Irish Sea on the Liverpool boat: "Round and round the deck I marched, fighting over every known thread of the intrigue. And when the last clumping sailor had pointedly called goodnight and gone below, I still marched on, round and round the deck mechanically. Once I stopped at the rail and looked down at the troubled waters, sliding, folding over, and turning past and, for a minute or more, I was nearer suicide than I shall ever be again." His detailed account of the affair is called 'From Chairmen and Committee Men, Good Lord Deliver Us'.

The Arts Council in January 1991 appointed Michael Haynes to succeed Kenneth Jamison as Director. The 'Sidelines' column of the February edition of the magazine *Fortnight* noted: "Surprise and controversy have surrounded the appointment of a new director of the Arts Council of Northern Ireland. It had been widely expected that the visual arts director, Brian Ferran, would get the job. Mr. Ferran, who is also deputy director, has a distinguished record as a vigorous promoter of Northern Irish artists. But the post has gone to an outsider—Michael Haynes, currently head of arts and entertainment with Hackney Council ... On the face of it his *curriculum vitæ* does not appear notably more impressive than Mr. Ferran's. And critics reckon it will take him ages to 'learn the language' of the north, given the intricate relations between arts and society. A local appointment would have made more sense at a time when the region's 'cultural cringe' is receding. If the Arts Council board is—with a few exceptions—the usual undistinguished quango, in one sense it has shown commendable liberalism. The good news is that it has appointed a black Englishman—the bad news is that it has not appointed a Derry Catholic."

Surprisingly, the job description had stated: "Practical experience in the arts and recent knowledge of Northern Ireland, though desirable, are not essential." Equivalent Northern Irish posts advertised by bodies like the BBC insist that extensive knowledge of Northern Ireland is essential. And in Scotland and Wales the importance of local knowledge and understanding is stressed as a matter of course. As Cyril Barrett observed in the July / August issue of *Art Monthly*: "So an accountant or assitant registrar could apply. Assuming that the candidate is in his or her forties and assuming that 'knowledge' means knowledge by acquaintance, he/she need not have been in the province for the past ten years or even know what is going on there. Stranger still, though the [Selection] Panel was delegated by the Board, its choice did not have to be ratified by the Board, nor did the Panel's choice of candidates have to be disclosed to the Board. Good Byzantine stuff."

In February Mary Holland wrote in her *Irish Times* column: "Whilst his background is not immediately relevant to his job application, it would do no harm in the broader political context if a Derry Catholic were appointed to a job with such a high profile." She went on to point out that recent surveys conducted by the Fair Employment Commission into employment patterns at the universities showed under-representation of Catholics in senior posts. She ended her article thus: "I must emphasise that I don't want to question the talents of the new director of the Northern Arts Council. However, one senior academic put the situation to me like this: 'At that level it's always possible to defend the individual appointment. When you get a choice between two candidates, both of them are likely to be well-qualified. The problem in Northern Ireland is that the decision always goes the same way. The job never goes to the person we can describe as 'the Derry Catholic'."

The appointment of its chief executive is probably the most important task that falls to members of a body such as the Arts Council. Michael Haynes and Brian Ferran were interviewed on 16 January. On 17 January, without ratification by the Board, the Council issued a press release which stated that the new director had been educated "at the Princeton University of New Jersey before coming to England to undertake his Masters Degree at Sussex University ... and a Practical Course in Arts Administration at the Polytechnic of Central London." The new director came to Belfast to meet his future colleagues. He talked with me for some thirty minutes. Two weeks later while I was recovering from an operation, pennies began to drop. I took a small rational step and phoned a literary friend in Princeton; then an academic friend in Sussex. With university records on computer the information came through almost immediately. I made a third phone call and asked a friend in London to contact the Polytechnic. I pursued my inquiries for three reasons: I had met the new director; I was well-acquainted with his most enthusiastic supporters; and, given past experience, a *débâcle* of some magnitude had been on the cards.

In late April the Council issued a second press release stating that "for personal reasons" Mr. Michael Haynes "did not intend to take up the post of Director"; and that the Board had met "and agreed to appoint Mr. Brian Ferran as Director." In the *Irish Times* the following day Anne Maguire wrote: "Mr. Haynes is understood to have withdrawn after his stated qualifications were questioned ... It is understood that the Council was informed a fortnight ago that he had not obtained these qualifications and subsequent to this, Mr. Haynes withdrew." In London the *Guardian* and the BBC's arts programme *Kaleidoscope* carried the same story. In Belfast the newspapers and local radio and television investigated nothing. It was left to Michael Haynes's local newspaper, the *Hackney Gazette*, to complete the hat-trick by reporting that the Polytechnic of Central London had not been running an arts administration course at the time he claimed to have studied there. By a proleptic irony, John Hewitt in his unpublished autobiography, *A North Light*, tells us about his move from Belfast to become Art Director of the Herbert Art Gallery and Museum in Coventry: "Some time later, I learnt from the Secretary to the University [Queen's] that the cautious Coventry folk had been checking that I was indeed a *bona fide* graduate."

In the June issue of *Fortnight* Jan Ashdown asked: "Is everyone just sitting tight and hoping the buck will pass? Why have there not been any resignations on the foot of such incompetence? What about accountability? What about the potential damage done to the arts world ... ? What about the personal damage done to those who had the courage to make their anxieties known ... ? Desire for secrecy and anger about disclosure are surely the marks of those more concerned to keep power grasped in tight wee fists than with the discovery of truth. Loyalty is no one's right, any more than is respect— both have to be earned, and one can only be a traitor to an honourable cause ... The arts are generally thought to be concerned with enlightenment, with the inculcation of civilised values and the development of moral understanding; artists are 'seekers after truth'. Is it too much to ask the institution that looks after the arts to remember these fundamental principles?"

Six months prior to this fiasco I had applied unsuccessfully for early retirement. I was told in a letter that "since a number of major issues of principle came into consideration, no action should be taken pending the appointment of [the new director] whose views on long-term staffing development should clearly not be anticipated." Out of the blue, in

March and a month before the new director withdrew, I was offered a reasonable deal and accepted it. The internal memo announcing my retirement informed colleagues that I would be leaving at the end of the month, in all of ten days' time. My sense of being given the bum's rush was mitigated by what my detective work had revealed (facts which, for legal reasons, were still unknown to my employers) and by my knowledge that I was considered a trouble-maker, a likely thorn in the side of the new regime, and better out of the way. (I gather that one member of staff had characterised me as "evil".) The Michael Haynes era was to begin without me, and, as things turned out, without him. When the carbuncle burst in April, I was pleased to be quoted by Anne Maguire in her *Irish Times* exposé: "I supported Brian Ferran before the appointment of Michael Haynes and after the appointment, despite charges of racism and sour grapes. He is a distinguished practising artist as well as a widely experienced arts administrator. He will make sure that the Arts Council is arts-led rather than dominated by bureaucracy. He will lead the arts triumphantly into the next century." And in the *Guardian* I described Ferran as "egalitarian and democratic by nature ... just the man for the job". A note of exuberance seemed appropriate. Apart from Jan Ashdown, no one else was saying anything.

Democracies are controlled by bureaucracies, networks of civil servants, vistas of decent people taking orders and saying 'Yes'. In a bureaucracy it is difficult to remain true to yourself. Facing the "dark tower", refusing to desert to the system, may help you to confirm your identity, but at some cost. By more than a coincidence, my first day of freedom saw the publication of *Gorse Fires*, my first collection in twelve years.

VII

As an arts administrator who tried to champion the individual creator and indigenous talent, I was pleased to accept an invitation to join the Cultural Traditions Group at its inception in 1988. Its aims, as I have said, are to encourage in Northern Ireland the acceptance and understanding of cultural diversity; to replace political belligerence with cultural pride. It has been rewarding to watch policy and action proceed hand in hand; to find management lines less rigidly drawn, bureaucracy kept under control; and to work with two or three creative civil servants—life-enhancers within the system.

In the Cultural Traditions Group we expect no quick returns. This is a waiting game. To plan for it in a disrupted social context like our own should not be beyond us. I think of when the British Labour Party came to power in 1945—many schools bombed out of existence; others needing renovation; half a million extra places required; a massive teacher-training programme to be organised; a radical Education Act to be implemented: and all to be financed out of a war-torn economy. This was achieved through the energy, optimism and experimentation of the new government's policy-making procedures. The policy-makers rubbed shoulders with the practitioners. Architects, civil servants, education officers and teachers were not kept in hermetically sealed administrative compartments.

With an initial budget from the government of £3,000,000 over three years, the Cultural Traditions Group has helped to steer grants to local publishers for good books (which would not otherwise be commercially viable) about history, politics, topography, folklore, local history; and has made down-payments, as it were, to independent producers for television and radio programmes of similar concern. The Ultach Trust has been established to help fund Irish language activities, thus grasping a political nettle. The Local History Trust Fund supports the work of many groups which make Northern Ireland probably the most vibrant corner of Europe when it comes to local history studies. A survey of place-names and the compilation of an Ulster-English dialect dictionary are underway. There are awards for those who have contributed to the cultural self-awareness of the society; and fellowships for young scholars. These are some of the projects which intertwine with the Education for Mutual Understanding and the Cultural Heritage strands now statutary in Northern Irish schools.

One of the founders of my old school, the Royal Belfast Academical Institution, was the United Irishman William Drennan. He might have been writing a charter for the Cultural Traditions Group when nearly two hundred years ago he proposed "the establishment of societies of liberal and ingenious men, uniting their labours, without regard to nation, sect or party in one grand pursuit, alike interesting to all, by which mental prejudice may be worn off, a humane and truly philosophic spirit may be cherished in the heart as well as the head, in practice as well as theory." The Group not only supports but has learned from enterprises like the John Hewitt Summer School which over the past five years has made a start by bringing together literature, local history, social and anthropological studies, languages, archaeology, the visual arts, topography and music in a spirit of interdisciplinary cross-pollination and under an ecumenical 'regionalist' umbrella.

The tragedy of Ulster brought the Group into being and continues to shape its deliberations. At a recent meeting I suggested that our aim should be to lift the community into consciousness and self-consciousness—the forming of a new intelligentsia, if you like—since it is the intellectual (and, indeed, the emotional) vacuum that makes room for the violence. We are involved in cultural preparation, a constellation of conversions, gradual processes which short-term thinking by the government could easily abort.

Sadly, this happened in the case of Conway Mill. The Conway Education Centre in West Belfast offers academic and recreational courses, social events and a wide-ranging cultural programme—including literary readings and debates. Its location means that supporters of Sinn Féin are inevitably involved in the enterprise. It was thus on allegedly security grounds that I was told to discontinue Arts Council funding of the Conway Mill cultural programme. I wrote a memorandum to the Chairman and Director and subsequently read it out to a meeting of the Board in December 1989. I argued that espousal of plurality could not be selective in this way; that withholding funds on the stated grounds strengthened the hand of the paramilitaries against moderating influences inside and outside the community; and that the ban not only damaged the trust which the Council's officers had built up on the Falls Road, but also tarnished their reputation for neutrality and thereby made it less safe for them to work in the area. A thoughtful debate ensued, but the Board did not follow my suggestion that they disobey Government. There was similar short-sightedness with reference to the Glor-na-nGael language-group in West Belfast.

Their funding has been restored, but its withdrawal threatened the work of Ultach Trust and the very idea of Cultural Traditions.

VIII

I find offensive the notion that what we inadequately call 'the Troubles' might provide inspiration for artists; and that in some weird *quid pro quo* the arts might provide solace for grief and anguish. Twenty years ago I wrote in *Causeway*: "Too many critics seem to expect a harvest of paintings, poems, plays and novels to drop from the twisted branches of civil discord. They fail to realise that the artist needs time in which to allow the raw material of experience to settle to an imaginative depth where he can transform it ... He is not some sort of super-journalist commenting with unfaltering spontaneity on events immediately after they have happened. Rather, as Wilfred Owen stated fifty years ago, it is the artist's duty to warn, to be tuned in before anyone else to the implications of a situation."

Ten years later I wrote for the Poetry Book Society about what I was trying to do in my fourth collection, *The Echo Gate*: "As an Ulsterman I realise that this may sound like fiddling while Rome burns. So I would insist that poetry is a normal human activity, its proper concern all of the things that happen to people. Though the poet's first duty must be to his imagination, he has other obligations—and not just as a citizen. He would be inhuman if he did not respond to tragic events in his own community, and a poor artist if he did not seek to endorse that response imaginatively. But if his imagination fails him, the result will be a dangerous impertinence.

In the context of political violence the deployment of words at their most precise and most suggestive remains one of the few antidotes to death-dealing dishonesty."

Patrick Kavanagh's famous distinction between the provincial cast of mind—abstract, imitative, sterile—and the parochial—close, familiar, teeming with life—applies to Northern Ireland in a particular and urgent sense. Terrified of Irishness—the cultural ideology of the Free State and then of the Republic—Unionists have clung to what after 1968 has increasingly become known as 'the Mainland', and to cultural importation. Those who depend on imports run the risk of themselves becoming exports. In his essay 'Crossing the Border' Hubert Butler describes "the more formidable of Ulster's enemies" as "those who keep quiet. 'Time is on our side,' they are saying ... 'The province has the artificial vitality of the garrison town and no organic life. If ever the pipeline were cut, it would perish.'" He ends his essay by suggesting that "Ulster would no longer be of value to Ireland if she were robbed of her rich history, her varied traditions."

Butler thought that reconciliation would not be complete in the South till it had happened in the North; and that it might develop out of regional loyalties. Meanwhile John Hewitt had begun his work of focusing our attention on Ulster's indigenous cultural resources. "Ulster," he wrote in 1947, "considered as a region and not as the symbol of any particular creed, can, I believe, command the loyalty of everyone of its inhabitants. For regional identity does not preclude, rather it requires, membership of a larger association." Hewitt did not seem too bothered as to whether that association might be a federated British Isles or a federal

Ireland.

Maurice Hayes used to tell a story which regained its currency after Down's victory over Meath in the Gaelic football all-Ireland final last year. Down's first major trophy was the National League in 1960, when they beat Cavan in the final. The captain, Kevin Mussen, brought the cup home to Hilltown in the Mournes—where it rested on the family sideboard. A few days later the local postman, a Unionist, an Orangeman and a 'B' Special, saw the trophy on his rounds and could not restrain his enthusiasm: "Jesus," he shouted, "we took it off the friggers!"

Here are the ambiguities latent in a sport played only by one section of a divided community and organised by a body which, because of its ideological overtones, is regarded with suspicion by another section. The story also illustrates the problems faced by those who reject the ideological message, but wish to recognise courage, effort, excellence or good performance—or who, in a close community, simply wish to share in the joy of their neighbours' success.

In Ulster cultural apartheid is sustained to their mutual impoverishment by both communities. W.R. Rodgers referred to the "creative wave of self-consciousness" which can result from a confluence of cultures. In Ulster this confluence pools historical contributions from the Irish, the Scots, the English and the Anglo-Irish. Reconciliation does not mean all the colours of the spectrum running so wetly together that they blur into muddy uniformity. Nor does it mean denying political differences. As William Faulkner said: "The past isn't dead and gone. It isn't even past yet." But reconstructing the past or constructing identities has too frequently been a purely propagandist activity in Northern Ireland. The

Cultural Traditions approach involves a mixture of affirmation, self-interrogation and mutual curiosity. To bring to light all that has been repressed can be a painful process; but, to quote the American theologian Don Shriver: "The cure and the remembrance are co-terminous".

1992

RIVER & FOUNTAIN
A Quatercentenary Poem

I

I am walking backwards into the future like a Greek.
I have nothing to say. There is nothing I would describe.
It was always thus: as if snow has fallen on Front
Square, and, feeling the downy silence of the snowflakes
That cover cobbles and each other, white erasing white,
I read shadow and snow-drift under the Campanile.

II

"It fits on to the back of a postage stamp," Robert said
As he scribbled out in tiny symbols the equation,
His silhouette a frost-flower on the window of my last
Year, his page the sky between chimney-stacks, his head
And my head at the city's centre aching for giddy
Limits, mathematics, poetry, squeaky nibs at all hours.

III

Top of the staircase, Number Sixteen in Botany Bay,
Slum-dwellers, we survived gas-rings that popped, slop-
Buckets in the bedrooms, changeable 'wives', and toasted
Doughy doorsteps, Freshmen turning into Sophisters
In front of the higgledy flames: our still-life, crusts
And buttery books, the half-empty marmalade jar.

IV

My Dansette Record Player bottled up like genies
Sibelius, Shostakovich, Bruckner, dusty sleeves
Accumulating next to Liddel and Scott's *Greek-English
Lexicon* voices the fluffy needle set almost free.
I was the culture vulture from Ulster, Vincent's joke
Who heard *The Rite of Spring* and contemplated suicide.

V

Adam was first to read the maroon-covered notebooks
I filled with innocent outpourings, Adam the scholar
Whose stammer could stop him christening this and that,
Whose Eden was annotation and vocabulary lists
In a precise classicist's hand, the love of words as words.
My first and best review was Adam's "I like these—I—I—"

VI

"College poet? Village idiot you mean!" (Vincent again).
In neither profession could I settle comfortably
Once Derek arrived reciting Rimbaud, giving names
To the constellations over the Examination Hall.
"Are you Longley? Can I borrow your typewriter? Soon?"
His was the first snow party I attended. I felt the cold.

VII

We were from the North, hitch-hikers on the Newry Road,
Faces that vanished from a hundred driving-mirrors
Down that warren of reflections—O'Neill's Bar,
       Nesbitt's—
And through Front Gate to Connemara and Inishere,
The raw experience of market towns and clachans, then
Back to Rooms, village of minds, poetry's townland.

VIII

Though College Square in Belfast and the Linen Hall
Had been our patch, nobody mentioned William Drennan.
In Dublin what dreams of liberty, the Index, the Ban:
Etonians on Commons cut our accents with a knife.
When Brendan from Ballylongford defied the Bishop, we
Flapped our wings together and were melted in the sun.

IX

A bath-house lotus-eater—fags, sodden *Irish Times*—
I tagged along with the Fabians, to embarrass Church
And State our grand design. Would-be class warriors
We raised, for a moment, the Red Flag at the Rubrics,
Then joined the Civil Service and talked of Civil Rights.
Was Trinity a Trojan Horse? Were we Greeks at all?

X

"The Golden Mean is a tension, Ladies, Gentlemen,
And not a dead level": the Homeric head of Stanford
Who would nearly sing the first lines of the *Odyssey*.
That year I should have failed, but, teaching the *Poetics*,
He asked us for definitions, and accepted mine:
"Sir, if prose is a river, then poetry's a fountain."

XI

Someone has skipped the seminar. Imagine his face,
The children's faces, my wife's: she sat beside me then
And they were waiting to be born, ghosts from a future
Without Tom: he fell in love just once and died of it.
Oh, to have turned away from everything to one face,
Eros and Thanatos your gods, icicle and dew.

XII

Walking forwards into the past with more of an idea
I want to say to my friends of thirty years ago
And to daughters and a son that Belfast is our home,
Prose a river still—the Liffey, the Lagan—and poetry
A fountain that plays in an imaginary Front Square.
When snow falls it is feathers from the wings of Icarus.